Jill is Viv and Rav's pet.
Jill has spots.

Can it be the pox?

1

Rav gets the vet.

The vet will visit Jill.

The vet gets in the van.

Will Jill get a jab?

No. Jill is not sick.

"It is not pox. It is wet bits!"

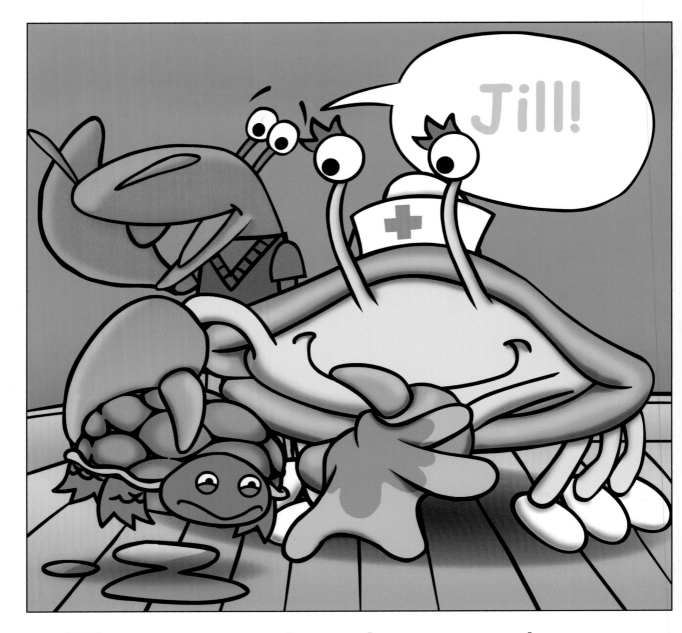

The vet rubs the wet bits off Jill.

Jill is well! The vet did a fab job!

The vet gets back into the van. The vet will go and visit the next pet.

Spelling and writing

Cover the words below. Say the first word (*vet*). Ask the child to repeat the word and tap out the phonemes in order with his or her fingers, saying each phoneme (*v-e-t*) and then writing the graphemes to spell the word. Repeat this with the other words.

vet   jab

wet   pox

Understanding the story   Ask the questions below to make sure that the children understand the story.

1 What is the matter with Jill? (page 1)

2 Who will visit Jill? (page 3)

3 Is Jill really ill? (page 7)

Assessment

Say the phonemes

Point to each grapheme in turn and ask the child to say the corresponding phonemes. Note whether the child is correct each time and go back to any incorrect ones.

Next, cover the graphemes. Say a phoneme and ask the child to write the corresponding grapheme. Prompt the child to write /l/, /f/ and /s/ in two different ways. Practise any that are incorrect.

j	ff	x	b
v	ll	w	ss

Read the words

Ask the child to sound out a word and then blend the phonemes and say the word. Repeat this with the other words.

will   vet   wax   jet